Cool Cookies

by Marilyn LaPenta

Consultant:
Sharon Richter, MS, RD, CDN

BEARPORT
PUBLISHING

NEW YORK, NEW YORK

Credits

All food illustrations by Kim Jones

Publisher: Kenn Goin
Senior Editor: Lisa Wiseman
Creative Director: Spencer Brinker
Design: Debrah Kaiser

Library of Congress Cataloging-in-Publication Data

LaPenta, Marilyn.
  Cool cookies / by Marilyn LaPenta ; consultant, Sharon Richter.
      p. cm. — (Yummy tummy recipes)
  Includes bibliographical references and index.
  ISBN-13: 978-1-61772-308-7 (library binding)
  ISBN-10: 1-61772-308-8 (library binding)
  1. Cookies—Juvenile literature. 2. Cookbooks. I. Title.
  TX772.L33 2012
  641.8'654—dc22

                              2011012738

For more information, write to Bearport Publishing Company, Inc., 45 West 21st Street, Suite 3B, New York, New York 10010. Printed in the United States of America in North Mankato, Minnesota.

073011
042711CGE

10 9 8 7 6 5 4 3 2 1

Contents

Making Cool Cookies 4

Getting Started 6

Light Oatmeal Delights 8

Granola Crisps 9

Crunchy Bran Drops 10

Thumbprint Jammies 11

Chewy Granola Bars 12

Pumpkin-Raisin Cookies 14

Banana-Apple Cookies 15

Giant Peanut Butter Treats 16

Chocolate Nests 17

Scrumptious Layered Squares 18

Chocolate Chip American Classic 19

Butter Form Cookies 20

Healthy Tips 22

Glossary 23

Index 24

Bibliography 24

Read More 24

Learn More Online 24

About the Author 24

Making Cool Cookies

Get ready to create some yummy cookies for your tummy! All the recipes in *Cool Cookies* make delicious treats—and you can bake them right at home.

The great thing about making your own food is that you know exactly what goes into it. Many **pre-made** cookies that you buy in the grocery store have ingredients to **preserve** them, which are not always good for your body. Often they also have more sugar and fat than needed. Many people already have too much fat and sugar in their diets—which can lead to **obesity** and heart disease. Use the ingredient substitution ideas on page 22 to make more heart-healthy versions of the cookies in this cookbook.

Remember that sweets should be enjoyed only once in a while! The cookies in this book have many healthy ingredients, but like most sweets, they also have lots of **calories**.

Getting Started

Use these cooking and safety tips, as well as the tool guide, to make the best cookies you've ever tasted!

Tips

Here are a few tips to get your baking off to a great start.

 Quickly check out the Prep Time, Cooking Time, Tools, and Servings information at the top of each recipe. It will tell you how long the recipe takes to prepare, the tools you'll need, and the number of people the recipe serves.

 Once you pick a recipe, set out the tools and ingredients that you will need on your worktable.

Wash your hands well with warm soapy water to kill any germs—both before and after cooking.

Put on an apron or smock to protect your clothes, and roll up long shirtsleeves to keep them clean.

 Tie back long hair or cover it to keep it out of the food.

Very important: Keep the adults happy by cleaning up the kitchen when you've finished cooking.

Be Safe

Before you begin, ask your parent for permission to bake. Then, make sure either Mom or Dad is around whenever the recipe asks that you:

 Use an appliance or sharp knife

Preheat the oven; put in or take out cookie sheets from a hot oven (Always use pot holders.)

 Heat foods on top of the stove (Keep the heat as low as possible to avoid burns from splatter.)

| PREP TIME | COOKING TIME | TOOLS | SERVINGS | INGREDIEN |

15 Minutes Prep Time **10-12** Minutes Cooking Time Tools **About 36** Cookies

Plus 2 hours to freeze the dough

Ingredients

Butter or cooking spray to grease the cookie sheets	⅓ cup white sugar	½ teaspoon almond extract
½ cup unsalted butter	1 egg	½ teaspoon salt
	1 cup **pre-sifted** all-purpose flour	½ cup jam or jelly (Choose the flavor you like the best.)

Steps

1. **Preheat** the oven to 375°F and then grease the cookie sheets.
2. In the large bowl, cream the butter and sugar with the electric mixer.
3. Crack the egg on the side of the bowl, letting it slide in. Then mix in the flour, almond extract, and salt with the electric mixer until dough forms.
4. Wrap the dough in wax paper and chill in the refrigerator for 2 hours.
5. After the dough has been refrigerated, break it into pieces and roll the pieces into 1-inch balls with your hands. If the dough is sticky, put a little bit of flour on your hands to make it easier to roll.
6. Place the balls of dough on the cookie sheets 2 inches apart.
7. Press your thumb into the center of each ball to make an indentation.
8. Fill each cookie with ¼ teaspoon of jam or jelly and bake them for 10-12 minutes, or until the edges are brown.
9. After carefully removing the cookie sheets from the oven with the pot holders, use the spatula to move the cookies to the wire rack to cool.

RECI

Jams and jellies come in lots of flavors, but the most popular are strawberry jam and grape jelly.

Special Tips for Cookies

Follow these tips to make your cookies even tastier.

 For crisp cookies, leave them in the oven a few minutes longer than the recipe says. For softer cookies, take them out of the oven a few minutes early.

 To grease a cookie sheet (so cookies won't stick), put a small amount of butter or other fat on a paper towel and rub it over the pan's cooking surface. Or you can spray the pan with cooking spray.

If cookies stick to the baking pan, use a wet spatula to remove them.

Place only one baking sheet in the oven at a time for best results.

Tools You Need

Each recipe in this book requires a stove or toaster oven, a refrigerator, and a few of these tools:

Fork

Sharp knife

Wooden spoon

Metal spatula

Large meat fork

Small mixing bowl

Medium mixing bowl

Large mixing bowl

Measuring spoons

Small plate

Measuring cups

Medium-size frying pan

9" X 13" baking dish

Baking sheet with sides

Baking sheet without sides

Electric mixer

Pot holders

Cookie cutters

Wax paper

Aluminum foil

Wire cooling rack

Cookie sheets (2 or more)

Rolling pin

Cutting board

Parchment paper

Double boiler or two pots, one of which fits inside the other

Light Oatmeal Delights

 15 Minutes Prep Time

 20 Minutes Cooking Time

Tools

About **48** Cookies

Ingredients

Butter or cooking spray to grease the cookie sheets

1 cup **pre-sifted** all-purpose flour

½ teaspoon baking soda

¼ teaspoon salt

1 cup butter, softened

1 cup confectioners' sugar

2 teaspoons pure vanilla or extract

1 cup old-fashioned oats

1 cup chopped pecans

*Optional: ½ cup dried cranberries

*Optional: 1 tablespoon confectioners' sugar for decoration

Steps

1. **Preheat** the oven to 325°F and lightly grease the cookie sheets.

2. Using the spoon, mix the flour, baking soda, and salt in the small bowl. Set aside.

3. In the large bowl, mix the butter, sugar, and vanilla with the electric mixer until smooth and creamy.

4. Pour the flour mixture into the large bowl and continue mixing with the electric mixer until dough forms.

5. With a spoon, gently stir in the oats and pecans. If you decide to use the dried cranberries, add them now.

6. Using a tablespoon, scoop up balls of dough and place them on the cookie sheets 2 inches apart.

7. Bake in the oven until lightly browned, about 20 minutes.

8. Carefully remove the cookies from the oven with the pot holders. Let them sit for one minute.

9. Move the cookies to the wire cooling rack with the spatula.

10. Let the cookies cool completely. If you like, sprinkle them with confectioners' sugar.

The number one use for oatmeal is as a breakfast food. The number two use is as an ingredient for cookies.

Granola Crisps

15 Minutes Prep Time   **8** Minutes Cooking Time   **Tools**   About **90** Cookies

Ingredients

Butter or cooking spray to grease the cookie sheets

1 ½ cups **pre-sifted** all-purpose flour

½ teaspoon salt

1 teaspoon baking soda

1 cup butter, softened

1 ¼ cups firmly packed brown sugar

1 egg

½ cup milk

2 cups natural whole grain granola cereal

1 cup dried cranberries

Steps

1. **Preheat** the oven to 375°F and grease the cookie sheets.

2. Mix together the flour, salt, and baking soda in the small bowl with the spoon. Then set aside.

3. Use the electric mixer to **cream** the butter and brown sugar in the large bowl until the mixture is light and fluffy.

4. Crack the egg on the side of the large bowl and let it slide in. Add the milk and **beat** with the electric mixer until blended.

5. Slowly add the flour mixture to the large bowl, blending well with the electric mixer until dough forms.

6. With the spoon, **fold** in the granola and dried cranberries.

7. Using a teaspoon, scoop up balls of dough and place them on the cookie sheets, 2 inches apart.

8. Bake each sheet of cookies, one at a time, for 8 minutes or until cookies are light brown.

9. Carefully remove the cookie sheet from the oven with the pot holders. Let it cool for one minute. Then use the spatula to place the cookies on the wire rack to continue cooling.

Invented in the 19th century, granola was the world's first cold breakfast cereal.

Health Tip

The best kind of granola to eat is one that is not sweetened with sugar. Read the label before buying.

Crunchy Bran Drops

 10 Minutes Prep Time

 **10** Minutes Cooking Time

 **Tools**

 About **18–20** Cookies

Ingredients

Butter or cooking spray to grease the cookie sheets

1 egg white

3 tablespoons white sugar

3 tablespoons honey

Dash of salt

1 teaspoon pure vanilla or extract

1 cup bran flakes (You can use other cereals, such as raisin bran.)

½ cup old-fashioned oats

½ cup shredded coconut

Steps

1. **Preheat** the oven to 350°F and lightly grease the cookie sheets.

2. In the medium-size bowl, **beat** the egg white with the electric mixer until stiff **peaks** form. It will take a few minutes. (Make sure the mixer is clean to get the best egg-white peaks.)

3. Add the sugar, honey, salt, and vanilla to the bowl and mix with the electric mixer until blended. Set aside.

4. In the small bowl, mix the bran, oats, and coconut with the mixing spoon. Then pour in the egg white peaks and continue stirring until well blended.

5. Use a tablespoon to scoop up balls of the mixture and place on the cookie sheets about 2 inches apart.

6. Bake for 10 minutes or until light brown.

7. Carefully take the cookies out of the oven using the pot holders. Let them cool for a few minutes before moving them with a wet spatula to the wire cooling rack.

A single worker bee makes about 1/12 of a teaspoon of honey in her entire life.

Health Tip

Bran is a great source of **fiber**, which can help maintain a healthy heart.

Thumbprint Jammies

 15 Minutes Prep Time*

10-12 Minutes Cooking Time

Tools

About **36** Cookies

*Plus 2 hours to chill the dough

Ingredients

Butter or cooking spray to grease the cookie sheets

½ cup unsalted butter

⅓ cup white sugar

1 egg

1 cup **pre-sifted** all-purpose flour

½ teaspoon almond extract

½ teaspoon salt

½ cup jam or jelly (Choose the flavor you like the best.)

Steps

1. **Preheat** the oven to 375°F and then grease the cookie sheets.

2. In the large bowl, **cream** the butter and sugar with the electric mixer.

3. Crack the egg on the side of the bowl, letting it slide in. Then mix in the flour, almond extract, and salt with the electric mixer until dough forms.

4. Wrap the dough in wax paper and chill in the refrigerator for 2 hours.

5. After the dough has been refrigerated, break it into pieces and roll the pieces into 1-inch balls with your hands. If the dough is sticky, put a little bit of flour on your hands to make it easier to roll.

6. Place the balls of dough on the cookie sheets, 2 inches apart.

7. Press your thumb into the center of each ball to make an indentation.

8. Fill each cookie's center with ¼ teaspoon of jam or jelly and bake for 10–12 minutes, or until the edges are brown.

9. After carefully removing the cookie sheets from the oven with the pot holders, use the spatula to move the cookies to the wire rack to cool.

Health Tip

When choosing a jam or jelly, look for one that is all natural with no added sugar.

Jams and jellies come in lots of flavors, but the most popular are strawberry jam and grape jelly.

11

Chewy Granola Bars

20 Minutes Prep Time*

10-12 Minutes Cooking Time

Tools

24 Bars

*Plus 3 to 4 hours to harden

Ingredients

Cooking spray

2 cups old-fashioned oats

¾ cup wheat germ

¾ cup sunflower seeds (You can use pumpkin, sesame, or other seeds instead.)

1 cup chopped pecans (You can also use walnuts, almonds, peanuts, or cashews instead.)

1 cup dried cranberries

½ cup dried apricots, cut up (You can use any other dried fruit, such as blueberries, raisins, or cherries.)

⅔ cup brown sugar

¼ cup honey

¼ cup maple syrup

4 tablespoons unsalted butter

½ teaspoon salt

Health Tip

Many scientific studies have shown that eating oatmeal daily may help reduce the risk of heart disease.

Steps

1. **Preheat** the oven to 400°F. Then line the baking sheet without sides with aluminum foil. Also line the baking sheet with sides with wax paper, sprayed lightly with cooking spray.

2. In one large bowl, stir together the oats, wheat germ, seeds, and nuts with the spoon. Pour the mixture onto the foil-covered baking sheet and toast in the oven for 10–12 minutes. During this time, stir the mixture with the spoon 2 or 3 times, watching closely to make sure that it doesn't burn. When the mixture is toasted, carefully remove the baking sheet from the oven using the pot holders.

3. Transfer the toasted granola mixture into the other large bowl. Mix in the dried fruit with the mixing spoon. Set aside.

4. Place a medium-size frying pan on the stove top. Pour in the brown sugar, honey, maple syrup, butter, and salt. Bring to a **boil**, stirring constantly with the spoon. Let boil for two minutes.

5. Turn off the stove. Using a pot holder, carefully pour the mixture from the frying pan into the bowl with the granola mixture. Stir hard with the spoon until it's mixed well.

6. Scrape the mixture onto the baking sheet that is covered with wax paper, and spread evenly.

7. Place another sheet of wax paper on top of the mixture and press down hard with the back of the spatula to make sure the mixture is flat and even. Remove the top piece of wax paper.

8. Let cool for 3 to 4 hours, or until hardened.

9. Once the granola is hard, turn the baking sheet over and push it out onto a cutting board. Remove the wax paper.

10. Cut the granola mix into bars. Press straight down with a sharp knife as you cut—don't try to "saw."

Sunflower seeds were first discovered in North America by Native Americans. They were considered an important high-energy food source.

13

Pumpkin-Raisin Cookies

15 Minutes Prep Time

13–15 Minutes Cooking Time

Tools

48 Cookies

Health Tip

Raisins make a great snack because they are fat free and **cholesterol** free.

Ingredients

2 cups **pre-sifted** all-purpose flour

1 cup old-fashioned oats

1 teaspoon baking soda

1 teaspoon baking powder

1 teaspoon cinnamon

½ teaspoon nutmeg

¼ teaspoon salt

½ cup unsalted butter at room temperature

1 cup white sugar

¼ cup light brown sugar

3 tablespoons honey

1 cup canned pure pumpkin

1 teaspoon pure vanilla or extract

1 egg

¾ cup raisins

¾ cup chopped walnuts

Steps

1. **Preheat** the oven to 350°F and line the cookie sheets with parchment paper.

2. Using a spoon, mix together the flour, oats, baking soda, baking powder, cinnamon, nutmeg, and salt in the small bowl. Set aside.

3. In the large bowl, mix the butter, sugars, honey, pumpkin, and vanilla with the electric mixer until well blended.

4. Crack the egg on the side of the large bowl, letting it slide in. Continue mixing with the electric mixer until well blended.

5. Pour the flour mixture into the large bowl and mix with the electric mixer until dough forms.

6. Using the spoon, stir in the raisins and nuts.

7. With a tablespoon, scoop up balls of dough and place them 1 inch apart on the cookie sheets. If you want puffy cookies, leave the dough as is. If you want flat cookies, press each ball with a fork to flatten.

8. Bake for 13–15 minutes or until lightly browned.

9. After carefully removing the cookie sheets from the oven with the pot holders, let the cookies cool for 2 minutes and then use the spatula to move them to the wire cooling rack.

Antarctica is the only continent where pumpkins cannot grow.

Banana-Apple Cookies

15 Minutes Prep Time

20 Minutes Cooking Time

Tools

36 Cookies

Ingredients

Butter or cooking spray to grease the cookie sheets

1 ripe banana

½ cup butter, softened

¾ cup brown sugar

1 cup oatmeal

½ cup **pre-sifted** all-purpose flour

¾ cup whole wheat flour

½ teaspoon baking powder

½ teaspoon baking soda

½ teaspoon cinnamon

½ teaspoon salt

½ cup chopped pecans

1 apple, washed, peeled, and diced

Health Tip

Many athletes eat a banana before a big competition, because the fruit provides them with lots of energy.

Steps

1. **Preheat** the oven to 325°F and grease the cookie sheets.

2. Peel the banana. In the large bowl, **mash** it with the fork.

3. To the same bowl, add the butter and brown sugar. Set aside.

4. Using the spoon, stir the oatmeal, all-purpose flour, wheat flour, baking powder, baking soda, cinnamon, and salt in the small bowl. Then add it to the banana mixture and mix well with the electric mixer until dough forms.

5. Add the nuts and the apple, stirring gently with the spoon.

6. Using a tablespoon, scoop up balls of dough and place them on the cookie sheets 2 inches apart. If you want puffy cookies, leave the dough as is. If you want flat cookies, press each ball with a fork to flatten.

7. Bake for 20 minutes. Then carefully remove the cookie sheets from the oven using the pot holders.

8. Use the spatula to move the cookies to a wire rack to cool.

As a banana ripens, the starch in the fruit turns to sugar. So the riper the banana, the sweeter it tastes!

Giant Peanut Butter Treats

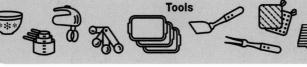

15 Minutes Prep Time

10–12 Minutes Cooking Time

Tools

8 5-Inch Jumbo Cookies

Ingredients

½ cup butter, softened

½ cup peanut butter

1 ¼ cups **pre-sifted** all-purpose flour

½ cup white sugar

¼ cup honey

½ teaspoon baking powder

½ teaspoon baking soda

½ teaspoon pure vanilla or extract

1 egg

Steps

1. **Preheat** the oven to 350°F.

2. In the large mixing bowl, combine the butter and peanut butter. Blend thoroughly with the electric mixer.

3. Add half of the flour, and all of the sugar, honey, baking powder, baking soda, and vanilla to the bowl. Then crack the egg on the side of the bowl and let it slide in. **Beat** all the ingredients with the electric mixer until thoroughly combined.

4. Add the remaining flour and continue beating with the electric mixer until dough forms.

5. Use your hands to make 8 balls of dough, each about the same size. Place 4 balls of dough, 2 inches apart, on each ungreased cookie sheet.

6. Press the balls of dough flat with the spatula. To flatten further, press a large meat fork in a crisscross pattern on the cookies.

7. Bake for 10-12 minutes or until lightly browned.

8. Carefully remove the cookie sheets from the oven using the pot holders and let cool for 2 to 3 minutes.

9. With the spatula, move the cookies from the sheets to the wire rack to continue cooling.

Although peanut butter is considered a kids' food, adults eat more of it than children do each year.

Chocolate Nests

*Plus 2 hours to harden

Ingredients

1 cup semisweet chocolate chips

1 cup butterscotch chips

2 cups Chinese chow mein noodles or bran cereal (It's best to use the twigs instead of the flakes.)

½ cup chopped peanuts or cashews

Optional: mini jelly beans for "egg" decoration

Steps

1. Line the cookie sheets with wax paper and set them aside.

2. With the help of an adult, melt the chocolate and butterscotch chips together on the stove in the top of the **double boiler**. Stir with the spoon until the chips are well blended and totally melted.

3. Mix in the noodles or cereal and the nuts. Stir with the spoon until they are completely covered in chocolate. Then turn off the stove.

4. Using a tablespoon, scoop up spoonfuls of the mixture and drop them onto the wax paper on the cookie sheets.

5. If desired, press jelly beans into the middle of each nest to create "eggs" in the nest.

6. Refrigerate for 2 hours or until hardened. Then enjoy your tasty treat.

Health Tip

Use dark chocolate instead of milk chocolate. It has more **antioxidants**.

A single chocolate chip can provide enough energy for an adult to walk 150 feet.

Scrumptious Layered Squares

10 Minutes Prep Time

30 Minutes Cooking Time

Tools

28 Squares

Ingredients

½ cup unsalted butter, softened

1 cup graham cracker crumbs

1 cup semisweet chocolate chips

1 cup peanut butter chips (Or you can use your favorite type of chip.)

1 cup shredded coconut

1 cup chopped walnuts (Or you can use your favorite kind of nut.)

1 small (14-ounce) can sweetened condensed milk

Steps

1. **Preheat** the oven to 325°F.

2. Melt the butter in the oven in a 9" x 13" baking dish.

3. Once the butter is melted, carefully take the baking dish from the oven using the pot holders. Stir in the graham cracker crumbs with a fork. Spread them evenly over the bottom of the pan.

4. Sprinkle one ingredient at a time on top of the graham cracker crumbs in the following order: chocolate chips, peanut butter chips, coconut, and walnuts. Do not mix the layers.

5. Pour the condensed milk on top of the ingredients, covering them entirely.

6. Bake for 30 minutes.

7. Carefully remove the baking dish from the oven using the pot holders. Set the dish on the wire cooking rack to cool.

8. Once cool, use the knife to cut the treat into squares.

Health Tip

Coconuts are very nutritious—rich in **fiber, vitamins,** and **minerals.**

Coconuts are used for many things other than food, including cooking oil, soaps, candles, and fuel.

Chocolate Chip American Classic

12-15 Minutes Prep Time

12-15 Minutes Cooking Time

Tools

48 Cookies

Ingredients

Butter or cooking spray to grease the cookie sheets

2 cups **pre-sifted** all-purpose flour

1 teaspoon baking soda

1 teaspoon salt

1 cup unsalted butter, softened

¾ cup white sugar

¾ cup dark brown sugar

1 teaspoon milk

1 teaspoon pure vanilla or extract

2 eggs

2 cups semisweet chocolate chips

Steps

1. **Preheat** the oven to 350°F and grease the cookie sheets.

2. In the small bowl, mix together the flour, baking soda, and salt with the spoon. Set aside.

3. Add the butter and sugars to the large bowl. Use the mixer to **cream** them together.

4. Add in milk and vanilla and continue mixing until blended.

5. Add one egg to the large bowl and **beat** with the mixer. Repeat with the second egg.

6. Now add the flour mixture to the large bowl. Stir with a mixing spoon to form the dough.

7. Add the chocolate chips and stir gently with the spoon.

8. Using a tablespoon, scoop up balls of dough and place them 2 inches apart on the cookie sheets.

9. Bake for 12 minutes for chewy cookies, or 15 minutes for crisp cookies.

10. Carefully remove the cookie sheets from the oven using the pot holders. Cool for one minute before moving the cookies with the spatula to a wire rack.

The chocolate chip cookie was invented in the 1930s when a Massachusetts innkeeper broke up a bar of semi-sweet chocolate and added it to her butter cookie dough.

Health Tip

Eggs are an excellent source of **protein**.

Butter Form Cookies

 10 Minutes Prep Time*

 8–10 Minutes Cooking Time

Tools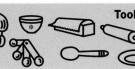

36 Cookies

*The dough must be refrigerated overnight.

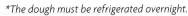

Ingredients

1 cup butter, softened

⅔ cup white sugar

1 egg

2 ½ cups **pre-sifted** all-purpose flour

½ teaspoon salt

1 teaspoon pure vanilla or extract

Colored sugar, sprinkles, fruit pieces, and nuts for decorating

*Optional: red and blue food coloring

Steps

1. In a large bowl, **cream** the butter and sugar with the electric mixer until it is light and fluffy.

2. Crack the egg on the side of the bowl, letting it slide in. **Beat** the ingredients with the electric mixer. Set aside.

3. In the small bowl, combine the flour, salt, and vanilla with the spoon. Then add it to the butter mixture. Mix well with the electric mixer until dough forms.

4. Separate the dough into three 4-inch balls. Wrap each ball in wax paper and refrigerate overnight.

5. The next day, **preheat** the oven to 350°F.

6. Sprinkle a dusting of flour on a clean work surface. Take one ball of dough from the refrigerator, and place it on top of the flour. Roll it with the rolling pin, from the center of the dough to the edge, until it is ¼ inch thick.

7. Put a small amount of flour onto a plate. Dip each cookie cutter into the flour, then press it into the dough. Cut out figures as close together as possible.

8. With the spatula, move the cut-out dough shapes to the ungreased cookie sheets.

9. Gather the leftover scraps of dough into a new ball. Then roll out the ball so you can cut out more shapes.

10. Repeat until no more dough is left. Then take out the next ball of dough from the refrigerator and repeat steps 6 through 9.

Steps (continued)

11 Decorate the cut-out cookies with colored sugar, sprinkles, fruit pieces, and nuts as you like.

12 Bake for 8–10 minutes. The cookies will be very light in color. Do not brown.

13 Carefully remove the cookie sheets from the oven using the pot holders. Let the hot cookies rest for one minute. Then move them with the spatula to the wire rack to cool.

Color It!

To make these cookies look even yummier, make them any color you want. You can turn the dough into the colors that represent your favorite holiday (Think red for Valentine's Day.), your school colors, or just your favorite colors. It's easy! Here's how you do it.

Health Tip

Scientists recently learned that eating eggs helps keep eyes healthy.

Patriotic Red, White, and Blue Butter Cookies

1 Divide one ball of dough into three smaller balls.

2 Put several drops of red food coloring on one of the balls of dough. Thoroughly work the food coloring into the dough with your fingers. Set aside.

3 Now work the blue food coloring into another small ball of dough.

4 Take a little piece of dough from the red ball, a little piece of dough from the blue ball, and a little piece of dough from the uncolored third ball. Roll the pieces into a larger ball.

5 Roll out the dough, cut it into any shape you want, and bake.

6 Gather the leftover scraps of dough into a new ball and repeat step 5.

Natural food colors are made from plants, spices, or other things found in nature. For example, red is often made from beet juice. However, it may also be made from insects!

Healthy Tips

Nutrition Facts

Serving Si... ...s (200g)

Amo... Per Serving

...ories 150   Calories from F...35

% Daily Value*

Total Fat 4g

Sat. Fat 3g

Trans Fat 0g

Cholesterrol 10mg   15...

Sodium 65mg   ...%

Total Carbohydrate 8g   0%

Fiber 0g

Sugars 8g

Protein ...20g   40%

Vitamin A 2% ...min C 0% • Calcium 20% • Iron 0%

*Percent ... ...alues (DV) are based on a 2,000
calorie di...

Always Read Labels

Labels on packaging tell how many calories are in each serving of a food, how many servings per package, and the amounts of various nutrients. By reading labels, you can see how many calories each ingredient adds to the recipe. You can also see how many calories come from fat and sugar.

Make Recipe Substitutions

While the recipes in this book call for wholesome ingredients, you can often lower the calories and get rid of **trans fats** and **saturated fats** by substituting one ingredient for another. For example:

Dairy

Milk: use **low-fat** or skim milk instead of whole milk.

Butter: use light butter

Sugar

Experiment with substituting some of the sugar that's called for with honey, molasses, maple syrup, or your favorite fruit **purees**.

Flour

Replace ¼ of the flour with a whole grain flour (bran, wheat, oats) to add more **fiber** to the recipe.

You may have to play around with these substitutions to get cookies with the taste and texture that you want.

Glossary

antioxidants (an-tee-OK-suh-duhnts) substances in certain foods that may prevent cell damage, which can cause disease

beat (BEET) to stir vigorously

boil (BOIL) to heat up a liquid until it starts to bubble

calories (KAL-uh-reez) measurements of the amount of energy that food provides

cholesterol (kuh-LESS-tuh-*rol*) a fatty substance people need to digest food; too much in the blood can increase the chance of heart disease

cream (KREEM) to whip butter and other ingredients together until the mixture is light yellow and creamy

double boiler (DU-buhl BOI-lur) two pots fitted together so the contents in the upper pot can be cooked or heated by boiling water in the lower pot

fiber (FYE-bur) a substance found in parts of plants that when eaten passes through the body but is not completely digested; it helps food move through one's intestines and is important for good health

fold (FOHLD) to mix using a gentle turning motion

low-fat (loh-FAT) food that has three or fewer grams of fat per serving

mash (MASH) to crush or pound to a soft pulp

minerals (MIN-ur-uhlz) parts of foods, such as calcium and iron, that a person's body needs to grow and stay healthy

obesity (oh-BEESS-uh-tee) a condition where a person is extremely overweight

peaks (PEEKS) pointed tops

preheat (pree-HEET) to turn on an oven and allow it to heat up to a specific temperature before using

pre-made (PREE-mayd) already prepared

preserve (pri-ZURV) to treat food with something, such as a chemical, so that it doesn't spoil

pre-sifted (PREE-*sift*-id) flour that has been dropped through a sieve or mesh screen before packaging to remove lumps

protein (PROH-teen) a substance found in plants and animals; essential for growth and for the repair of tissues

purees (pyoo-RAYZ) thick pastes made from foods that have been blended

saturated fats (SACH-uh-ray-tid FATS) unhealthy fats in butter, whole milk, cheese, and high-fat meats that can raise a person's cholesterol levels, increasing the risk of heart disease

starch (STARCH) a white substance found in foods such as potatoes and bananas

trans fats (TRANZ FATS) unhealthy fats in many pre-packaged foods that can raise cholesterol levels, increasing the risk of heart disease

vitamins (VYE-tuh-minz) substances in food that are necessary for good health

Index

almond extract 11

apple 15

banana 15

butterscotch chips 17

cereal 10, 17

chocolate chips 17, 18, 19

cinnamon 14, 15

coconut 10, 18

dried fruit 8, 9, 12–13

eggs 9, 10, 11, 14, 16, 19, 20

graham crackers 18

granola 9

honey 10, 12–13, 14, 16

jam 11

jelly 11

jelly beans 17

maple syrup 12–13

milk 9, 18, 19

nutmeg 14

nuts 8, 12–13, 14, 15, 17, 18

oatmeal 15

oats, old-fashioned 8, 10, 12–13, 14

peanut butter 16

peanut butter chips 18

pumpkin 14

raisins 14

sunflower seeds 12–13

vanilla, pure or extract 8, 10, 14, 16, 19, 20

wheat germ 12–13

Bibliography

Null, Shelly. *Healthy Cooking for Kids: Building Blocks for a Lifetime of Good Nutrition.* New York: St. Martin's Griffin (1999).

Trice, Laura. *The Wholesome Junk Food Cookbook: More Than 100 Healthy Recipes for Everyday Snacking.* Philadelphia: Running Press (2010).

Read More

Abrams, Michelle and Glenn. *The Kids-Did-It! Cookie Bookie: A Fun Cookie-Baking Cookbook for Kids, Illustrated by Kids!* San Diego, CA: Kids-Did-It! Properties (2009).

Karmel, Annabel. *Mom and Me Cookbook: Have Fun in the Kitchen.* New York: DK (2009).

Learn More Online

To learn more about making cool cookies, visit
www.bearportpublishing.com/YummyTummyRecipes

About the Author

Marilyn LaPenta has been a teacher for more than 25 years and has published numerous works for teachers and students. She has always enjoyed cooking with her students, her three children, and her three grandchildren. Marilyn lives in Brightwaters, New York, with her husband, Philip.